NUNC COGNOSCO EX PARTE

THOMAS J. BATA LIBRARY
TRENT UNIVERSITY

WHAT KIND OF GOVERNMENT?

LIBERAL - LABOR
COALITION vs.
TORY REACTION

by **TIM BUCK**

NATIONAL COMMITTEE, LABOR-PROGRESSIVE PARTY
73 Adelaide Street West, Toronto, Ontario, June 1944

JL 197 .L34 B8 1944

WHAT KIND OF GOVERNMENT?
Liberal-Labor Coalition vs. Tory Reaction

By TIM BUCK

THE news broadcast on the morning of June 7th stirred the hearts of Canadians from coast to coast. Their response was immediate and unqualified. In meetings, dedication services and public statements, they hailed the invasion and pledged their whole-hearted support to the men "over there." The response of our people, and the people of all democratic countries, testified to the truth of the words in General Eisenhower's stirring message to his troops at the start of the invasion:

"Soldiers, Sailors and Airmen of the Allied Expeditionary Force:

"You are about to embark on a great crusade. The eyes of the world are upon you and the hopes and prayers of all liberty-loving peoples go with you."

Never were truer words uttered. The hopes of the democratic people of the world and all their pent-up determination that the evil Nazi regime shall be destroyed went with our men to France that historic morning. The sentiments of working people were expressed perfectly by the workers of "Small Arms, Ltd." at Long Branch, Ontario. Under the leadership of their union (Local 519, United Electrical, Radio and Machine Workers of America, C.I.O.) they gathered in a shop meeting and dedicated themselves in unconditional support of the invasion troops in the words of the following pledge which they cabled to Gen. Eisenhower: "Hail your actions today and those of our gallant fighting forces. We pledge complete support in every conceivable manner to the cause you so aptly phrase in your Order of the Day. We workers say 'Give 'em hell, brother Ike'."

The spontaneous response of Canadians reflected the general realization that the invasion is the climax of the war. Fierce battles will have to be fought during the coming weeks. They may be costly. They will demand sacrifice on a scale such as we have not known of hitherto except through reports from the Soviet fighting fronts. They will require of us firm unity and unremitting effort in support of the invasion. They will require that the keynote of our activity shall be "Everything for the Fighting Fronts." What it will demand from us at home is trifling compared with the contribution being made by the men who are landing on the European continent. It will be given, freely, by all of us, because it is part of the price of United Nations victory—the indispensable key to peace and freedom for the building of a better post-war world.

Post-War Plans Are Necessary

We are now approaching the day of victory in Europe. Because of that, questions of post-war policy are becoming increasingly important. They are a vital part of the general strategy of victory. Mr. Cordell Hull, Secretary of State in the United States, emphasized this recently in the following words:

"The coming victory throws into clearer and sharper focus some of the tremendous tasks and problems which we shall face at the end of hostilities. Without relaxing our war effort in the slightest degree we must give profound thought to post-war problems and begin to take steps which will help to solve them. We must hold fast to a clear vision of the security and well-being for which we are fighting and work toward effective means to preserve them after they have been won."

Secretary Hull's warning is timely. The immediate post-war years will be a crucial period for all nations. For Canada they will be among the most crucial years of our history. The national policies developed during that period will determine the course of our national development for generations.

The government which will develop Canada's post-war policies will be chosen in the next Dominion election and we are approaching that election now. Every political party has been preparing for it for more than a year. We are now in the concluding stages of preparation. The provincial elections scheduled to be held during the next few months are part of the process by which the people are grouping themselves in favor of one line of policy, and government, or another. They are preparing to meet the issue which, after victory, will be decisive for the future of Canada.

The Issue of the Next Election

The question that the electorate will answer in the next Dominion election is: "What is to be the basis and the main line of Canada's national policies in the post-war years?" That will be the real question upon which the people will vote. The future of Canada depends upon their answer.

Whether we are to have a government with national policies to ensure full employment, a higher standard of life, better housing, continued growth of the Labor movement, far-reaching social reforms and international co-operation; or a government with national policies based upon backward-looking emphasis upon protective tariffs, low wages and empire exclusiveness, such as R. B. Bennett personified in the early nineteen-thirties. That will be the real issue of the elections, the only issue that will be decisive. Any importance that may be acquired by other issues will derive solely from their relationship to this basic question. No other issue will be important except as it is related to it.

The task of working-class leadership is to study that central question, decide upon the policies necessary to ensure continued progress for Canada, and continued gains for the Labor movement, then concentrate all possible energy upon electing a government which will carry such policies through.

What Should We Aim At?

What shall be the aim of the labor movement in Canada for the immediate post-war period? And, specifically, what sort of government should we try to elect in the forthcoming election?

There are people, some of them quite sincere, who argue that we should set our sights upon the immediate introduction of Socialism and direct our policies and propaganda for election of a government accordingly. Some of them even suggest that we should take advantage of the situation created by the war and advocate the establishment of Socialism now, while the war is on. That argument was carried to its logical conclusion by a provincial leader of the C.C.F. in a discussion with me some time ago. He argued that we must first establish Socialism in Canada and then develop a total war effort.

If such adventurism had been supported by a large percentage of the people it would have split the nation and disrupted the national war effort. The fact that it was repudiated by the overwhelming majority of the nation shows how little basis there is for "Socialism Now!" propaganda. Careful study reveals that **honest people** who support that propaganda are victims of "wishful thinking." There is no political basis for talk about establishing Socialism in Canada in the immediate future when only a small minority of the people are prepared to support its establishment. Furthermore, serious study of Canadian economy and the political opinions of our people shows that there is little probability of the majority of them becoming favorable to establishment of Socialism in the immediate future. This is easy to understand. Canada's economy has expanded rapidly during the past four years. Despite the fact that half of all that we produce is being consumed in the war, popular purchasing power has expanded and there has been some improvement in living standards and conditions. Nearly everybody is concerned about what is going to happen after the war but the overwhelming majority of people are willing to wait and see what happens after the fighting stops and "the boys come home."

But we cannot wait until the boys come home before

making our decision about the forthcoming election. Long before the last shot is fired the problem of post-war reconversion and economic re-adjustment will be upon us. The government which will introduce and administer the policies under which the re-adjustment will take place will be placed in office by the forthcoming Dominion election. The probabilities are that policies introduced by that government will dominate Canada's entire post-war development. Furthermore, it is quite evident that while only a relatively small minority of Canadians are as yet ready to abolish the capitalist system the majority of them **do want social reforms**. Workers want an assurance that there will be jobs, farmers want assurance that there will be markets at adequate prices, the men and women in the armed forces want assurance that adequate, nay generous, provision will be made so that every young man or woman who is demobilized shall have a good opportunity for re-establishment in civilian life, every section of the nation is acutely concerned as to whether or not popular purchasing power will be maintained.

The task of working-class leadership, and the problem of all democratic forces, in Canada is to secure broad agreement upon electoral policies which the majority of Canadians will support. It is evident that such policies cannot be based upon the idea of establishing Socialism after the next election. No, the policies which will win support from the majority of Canadians will be policies to ensure jobs, security, national health insurance, adequate old-age pensions, higher standards of prosperity for farmers, housing, a general increase in the national production and increased national well-being in the immediate post-war period. They must be policies broad enough to be acceptable to the thousands of men and women who desire the defeat of fascism and will support social reform but are not prepared to support the immediate establishment of Socialism. They must be proposals which can be carried through within Canada's present capitalist economy.

The Basis of Post-War Policy

Precisely because of the needs created by the war it is practical for the Labor movement to aim at such policies. There is a growing realization among all classes that such policies have been made necessary by the changes compelled by the war.

The stupendous increase in productive capacity made necessary by the war will make it impossible to dispose of all the products of Canada's fully employed industry and agriculture if there is simply a reversion to the cynical pre-war attitude of "devil take the hindmost." The terrible destructiveness of this war, combined with its drastic changes in world economy, render it absolutely essential that there should be organized co-operation and continuance of mutual aid in re-establishing world economy. The only basis upon which a stable peace and general security will be possible will be that of organized co-operation between the capitalist countries, headed by the United States and Britain and the Socialist Republics. That, indeed, will be a fundamental change from the policies which prevailed before the war.

Organized co-operation between the capitalist and socialist countries will ensure world peace but the alternative to it will be chronic world-wide crisis, sharpening international conflict and more war.

Such was the nature of the numerous changes and problems which confronted President Roosevelt, Prime Minister Churchill and Marshal Stalin when they met in their historic conference at Teheran. The task they set themselves in that conference was that of agreeing upon common immediate needs and aims; not of reconciling opposing ideologies. Facing realities as they did, they readily found common ground. The joint aims to which they pledged themselves in their famous Teheran Declaration are the things which had to be done if Hitler is to be defeated and the things which must be done if a breakdown of civilization is to be prevented when the war is over.

Their joint pledge points the way to recovery from the war's devastation, to elimination of the fierce international competition which has hitherto been one of the main causes of war, to the establishment of a world association of sovereign states, to large-scale expansion of world production and a general raising of standards of living.

The joint declaration signed by Roosevelt, Churchill and Stalin at Teheran is not a policy which they propose to impose upon the post-war world, it is a proposal that the democratic nations should co-operate in developing such policies at home and on a world scale. World policy can only be the combined results of national policies. The bright world perspective indicated in the joint statement of the three leaders will become reality only to the extent that the governments of the various countries introduce domestic policies in accord with its letter and spirit.

Our task is to help elect a government which will introduce domestic and foreign policies which strengthen the world trend towards international co-operation while bringing Canadians all the benefits that will accrue from policies based upon the Teheran Declaration.

For a Liberal-Labor Coalition

What sort of government will introduce the post-war policies we shall need in Canada?

A careful study of the situation shows that the choice is extremely limited. The only Dominion government, that can be elected, which will carry through policies of co-operation in mutual aid abroad and full employment with far-reaching social reforms at home is a government representing a partnership of Labor with that section of the capitalist class which is willing to support policies based upon the principles enunciated in the joint declaration issued at Teheran.

Announcement that the Labor-Progressive Party will campaign for election of such a government was received with expressions of amazement. But expressions of amazement gave way to either enthusiastic support or open hostility as thinking people realized that the line of action that we propose is the only one which will ensure continued progress for Canada and continued growth, and gains, for the Labor movement.

The need for a coalition in which Labor and capital are represented in terms of partnership is not peculiar to Canada. Several coalition governments have come into being as a result of the conditions created by the war and the changing tasks and basis of governments. The Churchill government in Britain is a coalition government. The National Liberation government of Yugoslavia is a coalition government. The Italian government is a coalition. The French Committee of National Liberation is a coalition. The Czecho-Slovakian government in exile is a coalition. There will be more coalition governments as more European nations are liberated and freely elect their own governments. In the existing state of political organization, and opinion, coalition is the only form through which governments can express the anti-fascist unity of all democratic people. Such a coalition will be necessary in Canada because: **Labor, alone, cannot carry through the policies that will be necessary in the post-war years and capital, alone, will not carry through such policies.**

Our proposal, therefore, is that the Labor movement (trade unions, labor political parties and other working-class organizations) should unite their forces to elect the largest possible number of members to the next Dominion House of Commons and should enter the elections with the declared aim of electing a government representing a Liberal-Labor coalition.

Why a Liberal-Labor coalition? The answer to that question is to be seen very clearly in the relationship of party policies and political forces in Canada.

Six parties have declared their intention of nominating candidates in the Dominion election.* A relatively small shift in the popular vote, or co-operation between two or more parties, may determine the government that Canada will have after the war.

The three major contestants for the government are the

---

* The Liberals, Progressive-Conservatives, C.C.F., Labor-Progressive, Bloc Populaire and Social Credit Parties.

Progressive-Conservatives, the C.C.F., and the King Liberals. According to recent polls of public opinion the people favor those three in about the following ratio: Progressive-Conservatives 29 per cent, C.C.F. 22 per cent, King Liberals 30 per cent.

There will be ocnsiderable change in the distribution of popular support before the elections but it is extremely unlikely that any one of the three parties will be able to elect its own candidates to a clear majority of the seats. There is a widespread and deep-seated sentiment throughout the Labor movement in favor of independent Labor representation. This powerful sentiment may even determine the outcome of the election. If it is misled into "opposition politics," it will simply divide the social reform vote and let in a Tory government—or a government representing a coalition of the Right. On the other hand, however, the powerful sentiment for independent Labor representation makes it possible to win a place for Labor as an independent partner in a government representing the unity of the overwhelming majority of Canadians around policies in accord with the new world perspective outlined at Teheran. Establishment of such a government, with Labor as a full partner in it, would open a new and higher stage of national progress in Canada.

The reader who feels that there is little danger of a coalition of the Right winning the next Dominion election should study the results of the general election held in Cuba on June 1st. The progressive movement is much stronger, relatively, in Cuba than is the case in Canada. There the national trade union movement and the workers' and peasants' political party are united on the political field and the retiring president, Batista, was a member of the progressive party; the Democratic Alliance. In spite of these powerful advantages the Democratic Alliance was defeated in the elections. The pro-fascist Dr. Grau San Martin was elected president and, within a few days of his election, he announced his intention of suppressing the United Socialist Party and the trade union movement. Post-election analyses by leaders of the United Cuban democratic movement reveal the fact that one of the main reasons for the pro-fascist victory was over-confidence on the part of the progressive forces. It is a serious warning of what could happen here.

Powerful interests in Canada see the trend towards international co-operation and social reform and they are determined to prevent such policies in Canada. The Progressive-Conservative Party is the main vehicle of their policies but their influence extends into almost every sphere of our national life. Their aims may be seen reflected in the speeches of Col. Drew, Prime Minister of Ontario, of Arthur Meighen, leader of the all-powerful Tory old guard, in the universal acclaim with which the Progressive-Conservative press greeted the imperialistic proposals by Lord Halifax in his Toronto speech.

The main line of progressive-conservative policy points clearly to an attempt to re-establish policies of the type by which R. B. Bennett intensified the effects of the crisis in 1930-35 to the rich profit of the monopolists in Canada. The Progressive-Conservative Party must be defeated in the next election if we are to have prosperity and democratic progress in Canada after the war.

An important section of the progressive movement feels, instinctively, that if Labor is to enter a coalition it should be with the C.C.F. A majority of the people who feel that way are quite honest, and sincere, but they have not faced the realities of the problem and thought it through.

The realities of the situation are as follows: <u>The C.C.F. leadership, and national and provincial conventions, sytematically rejects all proposals for co-operation with other sections of the labor political movement.</u> They reject, and sneer at proposals for maintenance of national unity after the war. They prophesy, with unconcealed gusto, economic crisis, chronic mass unemployment and social calamity after the war. Instead of co-operating in efforts to prevent such a disastrous development they look forward to it in the adventurist hope that "the worse things are, the better for the C.C.F."

The attitude of the C.C.F. leadership to the Teheran accord and to the principles set forth in it has been emphasized recently by its semi-official monthly magazine "The Canadian Forum." The leading article in the June issue of that magazine starts with the revealing statement that: "The outstanding characteristic of this war is its reactionary nature." That, "by contrast, the first world war was an inspiring revolutionary struggle." The writer argues through several columns of vicious anti-Soviet innuendo, which Hitler would certainly applaud, that the chances for democratic progress are slimmer than ever and that the main purpose of the Teheran accord is to prevent social change.

Members of the C.C.F. may argue that the writer of the article is not a national leader of their party but the fact will remain that he has stated in plain English what the leaders have been putting into diplomatic language for a long time. The entire thesis of the article could have been taken from the implications of an address delivered by Mr. M. J. Coldwell in New York some months ago. There is no prospect that the C.C.F. will even join in such a coalition as Canada will need.

The proposal for Liberal-Labor coalition expresses the realities of the situation. The Liberal Party is a capitalist party, one of the traditional parties of capitalism in Canada. But the overwhelming majority of Canadians still support the capitalist parties and the government which comes to power after the next election will be the government of a capitalist country. The point is that Mackenzie King is responding to the possibilities opened up at Teheran and, with a powerful Labor group as partner in the House representing powerful Labor support outside, he will go considerably further.

The King government which has organized and leads the war effort of which the nation is justly proud follows a line of policy much closer to that indicated in the Teheran declaration than any other except the Labor-Progressive Party. Mr. Mackenzie King's role in the London Conference of Commonwealth Prime Ministers was a truly Canadian battle for Commonwealth policies in accord with the spirit of the Teheran agreement. His consistent insistence that Canada's participation in a world association of states must not be conditioned by previous committments for narrower Empire aims deserved the enthusiastic support of every Canadian. Furthermore, it is a fact that the degree of national unity that we have achieved in the war has developed around the King government. Despite the weakness in its domestic policies, which reflect the sharp divergencies of Canadian opinion towards the war, it has retained support from important sections of workers, farmers, urban middle class people and big capital, in both French and English Canada, without which national unity would be impossible.

Through Victory to Progress

What nearly all working men want to be assured of when this war is over is a decent job. The desires of the great majority of our people could be summed up in similar terms. It is possible. It can be done.

Will such a coalition mean that the long struggle to develop independent parliamentary action is at an end? The answer of course is no! On the contrary, it will strengthen labor's independent parliamentary action. It will strengthen the possibility for united labor action around single labor candidates.

Does it mean that labor surrenders the idea of eventually electing a labor government? Of the eventual achievement of Socialism? Again the answer is no. It means exactly the opposite. The carrying through of such a policy would bring about direct labor partnership in the government in the most crucial period of our history; an independent partner whose role and influence will be determined by its independent parliamentary strength. It will not be a retreat, it will be an advance to full partnership in the leadership of the nation as part of the effort to make sure that the Bloc Populaire, padlock Duplessis, and the Progressive-Conservatives do not secure power.

United Nations armies are advancing to decisive battles in the war. When United Nations victory has been gained the people of the world will have an opportunity to advance towards a new world, a better world. The people of Canada must advance with them. The Labor-Progressive Party must help the great majority of our fellow-Canadians to understand the real meaning of Marxism in this electoral campaign by showing them what Marxism means: that is by helping them to achieve the world of peace, prosperity and democratic progress for which this war is being fought.

A government representing a Liberal-Labor coalition, pledged to policies in accord with the principles enunciated in the historic joint pledge issued from Teheran, will keep Canada in step with the social progress that we hope will be made all over the world when the menace of Fascism has been destroyed.

NATIONAL AFFAIRS
MONTHLY

The new Canadian magazine of Marxist opinion

Ever-increasing thousands of Canadians in all walks of life are turning to this outstanding new magazine. NATIONAL AFFAIRS gives them each month many interpretive articles on Canadian and world politics, economics and culture — written by the world's leading Marxists. As the official publication of the Labor-Progressive Party, it will help you keep abreast of swiftly-moving history.

ANNUAL SUBSCRIPTION—$1.50   —   PER COPY 1

Address your subscription orders to nearest
Labor-Progressive Party office, or direct to

73 ADELAIDE ST. W. - TORONTO 1, ONT.

SUBSCRIBE TODAY

Printed by Eveready Printers Ltd., 78 Wellington St. W., Toronto

Date Due

APR R 1982		MAR 2
	APR 1 0 1985	MAR 3 0 1994
MAR 1 5 1986		MAR 3 1 1998
JAN 3 1 1989		
APR 0 9 1994		APR 0 8 1998

JL 197 .L34 B8 1944
Buck, Tim, 1891-1973.
What kind of government? : Lib
010101 000

0 1999 00102914
TRENT UNIVERSITY

JL197 .L34B8 1944
Buck, Tim
What kind of government?

259097

CPSIA information can be obtained
at www.ICGtesting.com
Printed in the USA
LVHW080831170722
723605LV00030B/559